Break the Barriers
of Selling

Break the Barriers of Selling

DEEPAK D PRAKASH

PARTRIDGE
A Penguin Random House Company

To order additional copies of this book, contact
Partridge India
000 800 10062 62
orders.india@partridgepublishing.com

www.partridgepublishing.com/india

Thank you, my beloved wife,
Nandita who inspires me to write so the
world could know what I learnt

Preface

No institution in the world teaches you to be a salesman! It is either self-developed or requires you to be an apprentice, but where do you find masters? They are all either dead or dying! As the common eye sees it, this art is being eroded by marketing and logistics as a subject to learn. No offense to the professionals of marketing and logistics.

When you see a salesman, you do not see that he is here to give you something; you are sure he will take away something from you—not only your hard-earned money, but also your peace of mind. You see a salesman, and you think of an overbearing, flamboyant, talkative, over-smart bloke who has nothing better to do so he is selling. If you are a salesman in your family, you are considered as an outgoing, non-qualified, dominant, always-wanting-his-way person. And most of the time, you hear 'stop showing off your salesmanship with us'. Sadly, today salesmen are considered as people standing behind the counters of shops or people who direct customers to shelves at stores. That is the image which flashes when you say, 'Hey, look, a salesman!'

Then if these salesmen are being led by the owner/CEO of an outfit who himself is a salesman, then going will be from fine to good. If not, this bunch of highly motivated extroverts with the attitude of 'I will take on the world for you' and the bravado of 'I will make money for you to grow' they can be assured of a struggling, no-respect life as second-class citizens of the organisation. Mind you, the term *respect* is held in highest earning priority for the salesmen; reward comes later. Outfits today are more technically oriented than sales oriented; innovators are owning the businesses and not people of commerce, thus challenging the recognition of the salesmen.

All in all, being a salesman is no-more a career of pride, leadership, and of the brave. It is unfortunate! If these braves disappear in the world, who will make inventions and discoveries reach people, who will find buyers, who will demonstrate proof of concept, who will talk about concepts, who will make innovation reach the consumers? Please know that it all begins with a salesman!

Yes, this person is not required if products are already being bought, and if it is so, then you are busy competing and not innovating. Your products are one more in the line and have no exclusivity in them to demonstrate. If you are constantly innovating; you have exclusivity; you are required to reach out to new markets. You have a specific segment of market where your products should be bought, as first your product requires to be sold, and if so, then this salesman is your hero!

My intention for writing this book is to empower this dying community of braves, these alpha braves, who dare to go, meet strangers, demonstrate new innovations, and create markets to showcase the power of new innovations made to benefit people, mankind, and this world.

I was lucky to find a master and acquire the discipline, skills, knowledge, pride, and success and to have a family who supported my skills and talent, but I worry about the thousands of people who chose the career I chose and are suffering. I fear that these braves will become non-existent and people will suffer more by choosing the wrong products or maybe not even finding the products which they require as no one was there to support them;

the power of the product and the purpose of its innovation will be lost, and colour, glamour, and glitz will be the only thing left for the buyer's decision. So after these several years and witnessing the increasing suffocation of these braves, I chose to write for them and for people who will continue to require them.

My respects to every salesman in this world. I am one of you.

Acknowledgements

I, with all respect, acknowledge all who have inspired me—my teachers, family, colleagues, customers, friends, mates, and relatives who have made me what I am today.

I am indebted to my family for the patience, love, and care they provide me.

I am thankful to the management in my organization for an adventurous career and the opportunity to learn, to grow, and to give a purpose to contribute to the world, all in all giving meaning to my existence.

Thank you to all my rider brothers who kindle the spirit of freedom and brotherhood in me.

I thank all my apprentices, who support me and learn from me to grow.

I wish every person on this planet to be happy!

Introduction

There are several barriers which a salesman faces while selling. Most of them are either real or imaginary. All of them come from experience of the past, which is known, and from fear of the future, which is unknown. However, I believe all barriers can be overcome by using the right techniques of questioning and conversation between the buyer and the seller, which can be termed as *engagement*.

We, in these series of articles, will explore a few barriers that I have been able to overcome during my engagements of selling and would like to share with you. They will either help you if you practice or at least amuse you when they come your way.

Let's roll!

Part I

1. Why are you selling

2. What are you selling

3. Who are you selling to

4. How are you selling

5. When are you selling

Why are you selling

Mostly the art of selling and the need for high-impact salesmen are required by products which need to be sold and not bought. Let me qualify these two terms I have used—*bought* and *sold*.

A product which is *bought* today was *sold* earlier. Let me simplify it further: any product which sees the light of the world first requires to be *sold*. It has to be *sold* several times! This is because the benefits from the products are not implied or easily known. Then there are some kinds of products that require to be *sold* forever. This is because every buyer of such products sees its use differently or maybe the product is so versatile that it responds to variant needs of various buyers.

Salespeople helping the customer to buy in such an environment are commonly called salesmen, but they are actually extending their service and support for the customer to complete the process of purchase, and this is not selling.

In the case of *bought*, the buyer reaches out to buy the product; the buyer knows why he needs it and is willing to buy it at his known price. The buyer has learnt from his sources that his need is clearly addressed by the product. The buyer chooses from the variety of options which suits his eye and his pocket the most and procures it. In short, the deal is known and simple—he knows he needs it, he knows he can afford it, and he knows he will use it, so he goes and buys it. The expected delight of buying is a fantastic deal, which could be less price for the same product or the same price for more variety to select from.

Let us now see *sold*, the term which requires the hero of this compilation—the salesman. The term *sold*, when practiced, carves the salesman's name in the history of the product and leaves a lasting impression in the buyers' minds; many buyers who are 'sold to' benefit from the product. In the process of selling, the salesman enlightens buyers every time he *sells*.

A true, fast-growing career in sales is the domain of people who *sell* and not serve the customers who *buy*. The term *sold* is established when the seller reaches out to the buyer with what he has to sell. That is, the seller finds the buyer, introduces the product to the buyer, and one, few, many, or all the buyers agree to buy.

Many times the buyer does not buy the product but simply buys the seller's confidence. What the buyer buys is how the seller details the fitment of the product to the buyer's needs.

The compelling combination of the seller's product knowledge, his understanding of the buyer's requirement, and his ability to demonstrate the product's fitness by stating the benefits and displaying the product is what sells the product. Most of the time, new inventions and concepts require to be *sold*. In some cases, they are specific to a buyer's needs; in other cases, they are a need for many buyers.

However, only the seller knows which needs are addressed by his product. The buyers usually do not know what needs are getting addressed, and or many times the buyers do not even know that they need the product. This is when the product requires to be *sold* and cannot be *bought*. This is where the salesmen are required. This is when salesmen become the prime employee in their organizations and heroes of their buyers; this is because they know what they are selling.

In the *bought* environment, the buyer is commonly classified as *customer*. He knows what he wants, he tells you his need, you help him experience the product which addresses his need, and he buys. All in all, he knows his need and the product he needs, and you serve him.

In the *sold* environment, the buyer is commonly classified as *prospect*. He does not know his need, he does not know what product will address his need, you establish the need, you provide him the product to address his need, and he buys. All in all, he does not know his need and the product he needs, and you sell it to him.

What are you selling

First and foremost, the salesman needs to overcome himself being a barrier to the whole process of selling.

He first needs to know what is being sold. Why was it manufactured in the first place? How was it manufactured? What benefit does it provide? What is its purpose? What does it do? How does it work? What makes it unique? And whatever else a salesman can think of which will make him believe that what he is selling is the best of its kind and class.

A salesman needs to be well aware of the product he is selling. It is imperative that the salesman believes that it is a product he would buy and use if he was the buyer. Such conviction will enhance his reputation and image in the eyes of the buyer when the buyer pays him for the product. This can come true if and only if the salesman knows the rigours and pains his product goes through before reaching his hands to be sold. The salesman has to trust the benefits the product offers, and he has to understand the concerns a buyer experiences after he buys; he has to be knowledgeable of the environment he is selling to, the landscape of the area he is selling in, and the domain knowledge of the product he is selling.

All this can happen only if the salesman believes in the benefits the product can provide to the buyer and can demonstrate his product to the buyer. When the buyer sees the salesman as the master of his game (i.e. his product), that is when the buyer realizes that it is not the selling of the salesman or the salesman that the buyer is paying for. The buyer realizes that he needed or needs the product, and that is what he will pay for—his need. It is important that the salesman knows his product well and also masters every aspect of his product, each of its component, its purpose, and what it precisely delivers.

A salesman should not only know how to state and present the product's benefits but should also know how to demonstrate the product by his very own hands. A salesman should not require another expert or entourage to demonstrate or provide the experience to the buyer.

Every salesman should practice or train himself well before he delivers his act to his buyers.

Many salesmen, in their pride never learn and know more about the product they are selling, its benefits, and how it works. Thus, they become fools in selling tools and devices or even bigger fools by smart-talking the buyer.

Trust me, the buyer knows what the salesman is doing, and the buyer only sees it as entertainment; he passes or overcomes the salesman by getting amused or amusing the salesman by postponing his intention to buy.

Buyers like to know what they are buying and appreciate it if the seller can tell more than what the buyer already knows. A salesman's effectiveness in selling is very crucial for every buyer to take his decision to buy.

Let us look at a situation here. Most of us have been on school excursions when we were young; even now, we go for holidays with our friends and families. If the excursions or holidays happen to have sightseeing involved (which has immense value to your knowledge—for example, a historical site or science centre), we all prefer to hire a guide to know more intricacies of the place or the stories of glory attached.

The experience with a guide to rely on is different; the guide makes it more informative, more fun, and more interesting. The guide offers you the comfort of 'I know'. Similar is the role of the salesman; he is a guide to his buyer. This can happen only if the guide—the salesman—has better practice and more knowledge of what he is demonstrating to sell than the buyer.

Who are you selling to

Now that we know why we have to sell and what we are selling, the next question to know and reflect on is how the product becomes a need for the buyer. In simple words, who is your buyer? Or even simpler, who are you selling to?

Salesmen in haste forget to evaluate the customer. Salesmen love to meet people; the best attitude a salesman can have is that even if the buyer does not buy, the salesman will know one more person in this world and also possibly learn about another kind of business and business processes in engagement. If the buyer buys, it is an achievement to be proud of indeed.

The salesman should prepare certain questions which he should always ask the buyer soon after introductions.

These questions can be standardized for the products that the salesman sells. The buyer's answers to these questions should not only tell the salesman more about the buyer and his needs but also break the ice between the seller and the buyer.

So what are these questions? How should they be framed? How should they be asked? The seller should begin the engagement process by greeting the buyer. He should proactively introduce himself and the organization he represents and detail the purpose of the discussion. At this stage, the seller should also hand over his visiting card to the buyer. The visiting card is an important device to use as it will constantly remind the buyer of the seller's name and the organization he represents, establish identity, and is a very useful recall device left with the buyer.

Next, a salesman should ask for a seat and permission to take notes in his personal diary, which the salesman would like to record for reference. Finally, the salesman should seek permission to ask questions to know the buyer so the discussion could be relevant and avoid waste of each other's precious time. The next step is the conversation of questions between the seller and the buyer.

The conversation of questions should be more like a talk show we see on televisions, and it should not be a typical job interview or an examination by test papers or a viva. The seller should ensure an easy environment and keep a polite tone. He should smile often, and his expressions should be intriguing. He should acknowledge the answers and maintain constant clear notes.

Now you may ask what should be the questions. Well, the questions should be in the context of knowing the nature of the buyer—what constitutes his organization or family, what are his preferences, what are his needs as identified by him, what is on top of his mind to purchase in the current time, and what would he love to spend his money on today? If he knows anything about the product you deal with, what does he know about what your products do? Does he know anyone who uses your products? How did he become aware of your products?

Now each of the responses should be recorded not on a sheet but in the salesman's diary, with name of the client on the top. The page should be marked 'To know the buyer'.

Then comes the next phase of questions, which are directly relevant to establish the need of the product for the buyers—what is he using or consuming today, what are his likes and dislikes of what he is already using, and what changes or improvements does he seek in the current product?

These two phases of questioning should reveal sufficient information about the buyers, which will help the salesman to position his product, address the needs, and demonstrate the experience to the buyer. And yes, while the buyer is responding to questions, the salesman needs to make a note of statements which the product resolves, make a note of the statements of the buyer which he wants to see resolved. I like to call them 'hook' statements.

The 'hook' has the same purpose as the one used in fishing. If you have not gone on a fishing expedition in a stream (not a pond, a lake, a sea, or an ocean), please do experience it. Such fishing is also known as angling. You in this expedition will learn so much more about selling—the water body being the market, fishes being the buyers, and you being the man out to fish. To motivate you, some keywords in fishing are *patience*, *persistence*, and *consistency*. Key needs are fishing rod, hook, bait, and fishes.

How are you selling

This brings me to the next topic: what is the equipment that the salesman must carry to make the sale? Has he got a fishing rod, bait, and hook for fishing? Has he prepared the kit to sell.

We have heard several times in various aspects of life that preparation is the key! Before a salesman begins a day of sale, he has to ensure that he has prepared well. The salesman has to ensure that all his equipment is with him—his visiting cards, diary, pen, product pamphlets, product tech-specs document, sample of the products, testimonials, presentation of the organization he represents, and the presentation of the product and its benefits for all the relevant audiences he is expected to meet or probably meet.

Who are these audiences the salesman needs to know and be prepared for? In any sale, there are *influencers*, *beneficiaries*, and *buyers*. Let us actually understand the difference. This is where the biggest barrier to sale is faced. The right to argue and reject the purchase is amongst these three audiences. The salesman should always identify them by name and be prepared to address in person these three audiences in his engagement of sales.

The *influencer* is a person who gains indirect benefit or loss from the sale. He is also considered the subject matter expert by the buyer. The irony is that the buyer sees him as an unbiased adviser while he is limited to his knowledge and preferences, which the salesman will require to address. This person is the most invisible identity; he could be a friend, colleague, industry expert, user, peer, or even a relative. The salesman should always investigate to know who the influencer is and engage with him for his acceptance.

Then when I say *beneficiary*, who would be this person? This is the person who will actually consume or operate the product and is not necessarily the *buyer*. For example, I recently bought a desktop PC, and before buying, I evaluated it, spoke to a few people who I knew were users, spoke to my tech-savvy friend, made the appropriate queries to the seller, and enquired about the after-purchase services available. It was my son who had to operate it; thus, my son becomes the *beneficiary*. All my queries, decisions, and affirmations would have emerged from his needs, and so it is important that the *beneficiary* is also identified and appropriate engagement is done with the *beneficiary* so he too agrees to the buyer's decision or can support the *buyer* to make the decision.

Then lastly, there is the king, the *buyer*; in the above case, it was I. The *buyer* is mostly the person who will sign on the affirmation to buy, the person who will make the final decision to pay, the person who will be accountable for the money to be spent to buy, and the person the salesman has to mandatorily engage with by all means. Till the salesman engages with him, it is a sale by chance and in a way *bought* and not *sold*. He is the king!

So in the conversation with the buyer, the salesman is required to identify the *buyer*, the *beneficiary*, and the *influencer*. The salesman has to be prepared to engage with each of them, and it is not *sold* till he has engaged with the buyer as only then can he determine whether the product is *sold* or *bought* or *not yet*.

So what does *engagement* mean? *Engagement*, as the word suggests, is meeting the buyer face to face, there is eye contact between the buyer and seller. As I said in the beginning, if you *sell*, then you have to reach out to the buyer and engage with him. If your product is *bought,* mostly it is the buyer who reaches out to buy. Businesses usually have to be reached out in order to sell to them the products and services they need to operate it. Consumers mostly reach out to the seller. What you use in the engagement is the knowledge and equipment.

Prepare to engage, reach-out to engage and engage are the keys to the three locks in the *sold* environment. Identification of the influencer, beneficiary, and buyer, along with appropriate engagement with them, are required for products to be sold.

When are you selling

There is a saying that states strike when the iron is hot. When products are bought, the buyer is the hot iron and takes the effort to buy, the seller is the striker, and your products to sell is the hammer. However, in the case of *sold*, it is a challenge to know when the iron is hot, i.e. the time when the customer is ready and will buy the product. This is a very important step to know and take when the products are sold.

When does the seller tell the buyer, 'Please give me the order. When can I deliver the product to you?' Now, if the salesman tries to push the sale when the buyer is focused on other compelling matters, he will lose the sale. This is not because of the reasons known to the salesman but will be because of the reasons which are only known to the buyer. So the salesman should never push too hard for the payment or order but should rather spend his energies and time in engaging with the buyer to demonstrate the buyer's need and resolve his queries.

While selling, the salesman has to ensure that the buyer has time carved out for the engagement and is not preoccupied with other matters, general or critical; in either case, if the salesman does not have the attention of the buyer, the sale and time spent will be lost. A salesman should make an excuse and ask for another appointment to meet, ensuring that the seller understands the situation and is more than willing to support his buyer. Be reassured that in the next appointment the buyer will ensure all the time in the world for you as one thing is established to the buyer—that 'this salesman cares'.

The salesman has to ensure that he is enthusiastic about meeting the buyer. The salesman has to be excited to demonstrate the buyer his products. he salesman has to be eager to discuss his offerings with the buyer. Nothing can be more important to him than the time the buyer has appointed and given. There can be no phone calls, no emails, and no loss of concentration during this time. The entire focus in this time should be on getting to know the buyer and establishing his need.

If for any reason the salesman is distracted or cannot concentrate, it is better to make a timely call and postpone the meeting, citing appropriate reasons, and there and then fix up another time to meet. The buyer cannot or does not need to understand or know what has kept the salesman preoccupied and will see the engagement as the best of whatever the salesman delivers to sell. However, the irony is, the salesman will have to understand the buyer's preoccupation and also appreciate and accommodate. After all, the buyer is the king and will remain the king after he becomes the customer too.

Due to the pressure of time and lack of concentration, the haste of selling creeps in. This haste kills the sale or defers the decision to buy by the buyer for an unknown period. This situation is usually blamed on the buyer but is mostly created by the salesmen. As we have already read above, it is the seller who has to appreciate the time of the buyer and keep the patience. This haste and impatience is a result of the urgency to close the targets or, even worse, less number of prospects in hand.

A salesman has to always ensure that he spends most of his time in creating prospects and much lesser time to converting prospects to customers. Unfortunately, most of the salesman's time is spent in follow-ups for decisions, following up with order processing, payment collections, and deliveries. The salesman has to ensure that 50 percent of his time goes into prospect building, 25 per cent into conversions from prospect to customers, 10 per cent into preparations, and 15 per cent into learning new skills, training himself on the latest equipment, and acquiring domain knowledge.

Part II

1. Hygiene

2. Conversation

3. Demonstrating

4. Benefits

5. Negotiating

Hygiene

A man in a crisp light-coloured pinstriped shirt, with a tie to make a statement, grey creased pants, a belt to match the shoes, socks to blend, black shiny shoes with laces, hair combed, a whiff of aftershave, a naughty smile on the face, a walk of confidence, a pen in his shirt pocket, a briefcase in his hand, and a watch to tally—isn't this what comes to mind when we say '*salesman*'?

Salesmen are expected to be a high-energy, optimistic, and savvy group of people. Their walk is energetic, their aura and presence can be felt in their surroundings, and they have a freshness in them. They stand out like a fruit tree in the middle of the desert. All this, comes from the expectations of their buyers. Let us understand why.

If you do not respect yourself, how will your buyers respect you? It all starts from here. What does *respect* here mean? While the world will appreciate your knowledge and skills, before that, what they see is *you*! The question we have to keep asking is, are they pleased to see you? Or do they wriggle their nose when they see you? Do their eyes sparkle, or do they see you as one more amongst the thousands? Do you electrify the atmosphere around you? Most of us—due to lack of discipline, burden of expectations, and beating of time—forget what we are and how are we presenting ourselves. This results into a non-starter of engagement with your buyer.

Today, to be dressed casually and unshaven is savvy. With newbies, it is a statement of the 'new order'—as in the times of old, it was the hippies. The techies and thinkers have also caused this change, the attitude of 'No matter what you wear, what you invent or create is what I want'. But this cannot apply to the pedigree born of sales.

For people who have a career in sales, their personality and presentation of self *is* the first impression they leave about themselves and what they represent and is also a statement of who they are.

Salesmen are like warriors who go out in the battle arena to win and bring their winnings home in all pomp and glory. They win the battle with their enthusiasm, focus, strategy, wit, might, weapons, and swiftness. All this requires discipline, training, and preparation. To dress up for the day is to prepare for the battle; dress up to make a statement of your might and preparedness.

The question is, how are you dressed up for meeting strangers today? When a stranger meets you, what will he see first—a crisp, neat, smartly dressed salesman who has enthusiasm in his walk, happiness on his face, and confidence in his eyes? When the customer sees you, can he say, 'Wow, here goes a man who has something I want, I want to talk to him'?

Like a white coat and stethoscope is to a doctor, formal dressing and bag is to a salesman. Are you dressed formally and prepared to engage anytime and every time?

When the customer sees you for the first time, this is the image which flashes in his head forever about you and who you represent; it creates a perception in your customer's mind which should be in your favour. He should say, 'All my sales team should be dressed like him.'

Invest in a good set for formal clothes; they are your identity and statement of your personality and the respect you demand. Invest in yourself!

Imagine a jean-clad strange person with a loud-colour shirt, unshaven, and with swinging hands, walks up to you and stands in front of you. In that very snap of the moment, what will you think? Exactly! This is the impression a buyer builds about you. If it is not in your favour, you will continue to struggle to break your image than having favourable conversation about where you come from and what you have. Your buyer has already decided who you are; now to him, you are a casual and easy person and cannot be taken seriously. No offense to casual dressing, but one thing is for sure—you will not be seen as a serious salesman who will be worth giving money for something you have to give to your buyers.

There are some salesmen with unpolished shoes, sweaty hands, body odour, smells of just-had-a-garlic-filled-snack, broken buttons all adding to their personality and making a repulsive statement—Stay away!

You as salesmen have to be careful about your appearance all of day; every time a customer meets us, it is his first impression of us, and he does not have a clue how your day has been and expects you to be 'fresh out of the oven' to engage with.

Then I spoke of the briefcase. What does the briefcase have—dirty, unfiled papers; dirty towel; broken, leaking pen; tattered notepad; torn diary; a plastic box of visiting cards? Or do you carry visiting cards in the shirt pocket along with a pen to impress with? Do you carry a neat, ruled notebook/diary to take notes on? Are your product details and profile nicely stacked?

All in all, are you prepared for the battles of the day?

Conversation

To talk and being talkative is appreciated as a quality in sales; to be witty is considered as being a smart salesman. Don't we all hear when we meet our acquaintances that 'you talk so much, you must be in sales'? Is it true? While speaking is important, is being talkative a quality? I do not think so.

Then some of us learn the lesson of listening and confuse it with 'Silence is golden'. We listen but remain quiet. Is that good? I do not think so; either we will talk, or we will go dead silent. Not okay.

What we need to do is have a conversation, 'a talk, especially an informal one, between two or more people, in which news and ideas are exchanged'.

Two or more people having a mutually beneficial discussion in which all parties participate to come to an agreed conclusion can be a fine example of a conversation.

We in selling are required to build agreement and confidence in what we are selling so that our buyer will buy; it has to end in an exchange/trade between two people. This can result only when two people build the momentum over the subject of purchasing the product/ service being sold. The buyer builds his confidence by exposing what he needs; this will happen when the salesman asks the questions to know his needs. Then the salesman demonstrates how the buyer's needs are fulfilled and to what extent, which is registered by the buyer by asking his questions and getting responses.

Such actions build a conversation between the parties, leading to clarity and confidence, which are the catalysts to making a decision.

A conversation cannot be made if it is mugged; it cannot be made if you have trained yourself to present. A conversation flows naturally as it builds appreciation for each other and builds and exudes confidence on the subject, agreements, and disagreements. It establishes an environment of trust and knowledge. It allows both the salesman and the buyer to know more about each other and appreciate each other, constructing a relationship.

The salesman should be at ease and in comfort during the approach. While conversing should be formal, body language should exude calmness and concentration. The salesman should make his buyer feel at ease and establish no compulsion to decide but an environment to give and acquire knowledge, leading to an acquaintance at least, if not a customer yet. The salesman should have the confidence that if not now, then some time later with something else. Once the buyer is comfortable and is willing to know more about the product, with no obligation, he will start asking questions and discuss his expectations, which is what you want to establish to make your sale effective and his requirement met.

What one usually sees though is that salesmen are trained in what to say; they meet the customer and blabber everything they have mugged and ask the customer to buy. The fear they engage with is that 'if the customer asks a question I do not know the answer to, he will win, and I will lose'. Such episodes become an engagement of a 'game' and not a sale.

The salesman will introduce himself, give a pitch about his company and the product he sells, pull out a brochure, explain the features mentioned in the brochure, tell why it is a great product and how affordable the product is than its competition, and ask the buyer if he is interested in buying! How more parched can it get? This way, it can never be fun to sell and buy.

The salesman should not make it a one-sided discussion as it is not a game of win and lose, but a win-win; buyer wins the product, and the salesman wins the sale. And if at all it is a game for you, then it has to be that your buyer wins the product and you lose the product. The money taken is income for services rendered and not a sale.

Conversation will help establish collaboration, togetherness; it will act as a bridge between you and the customer to reach a decision—a decision to buy what the salesman is selling.

Build conversation to sell; do not blabber your over-smart, rock-star pitch. Your buyers do not want a speech; they want your product and want to know why they should buy and why they should buy from you.

Conversation should happen to listen, restate your understanding, and then convey your opinion. Receive acknowledgement and keep building it up till agreements and disagreements are established and both seller and buyer are able to conclude the conversation with an outcome to proceed, to converse again, or to abandon the conversation.

Converse to be acquainted, to know more about your buyer, and to tell about yourself; the sale will follow!

Demonstrating

If you are confident of your product, you will demonstrate your products; if you love it, you will flaunt it! The power of demonstrating is amazing; demonstrating what you have allows your buyer to feel his need getting fulfilled. It allows him to experience fulfilment, and thus the willingness to purchase and pay the price is far greater. When you demonstrate, you not only establish what the buyer is buying but it is a statement of why he should buy from you. Demonstration exudes confidence, which comes from command, which further comes from practice, which further comes from knowledge. Buyers pay for this confidence!

Most salesmen believe they can sell anything, so they need not know anything about what they are selling as the customer buys because they sell. It all starts right at the time of job interview of a potential salesman during recruitment. The most commonly asked question at the time of interviewing the salesman candidate is 'this is a pen, sell it to me'. The candidate does some smart talking and bullshits about the pen, and he is hired; the message is loud and clear: 'We have hired you to talk bullshit to our customers.' And that is exactly what he does. No, sir, this is why sales is tough and the salesman is unable to sell.

You have to be clear to the sales team that they have to know the uniqueness of the product, they have to use it to experience it, they have to master it to be able to demonstrate it to their buyers, and they have to master it sufficiently enough that they can even customise the demonstration on the fly based on their conversation with the buyer. Unless you know why the product is made, how the product is made, and what the differentiator is, you will not be able to sell it; if you demonstrate it and make your buyer feel it, the sale is faster and easier.

Mostly you will notice that when your buyers are not aware of your products but you do become aware that they need your products, they will want to 'feel' your product, and they will want a brief experience of your product. It is important that you reconcile the fact that everyone will not like your product and thus only some will buy what you are selling. Then you should sell only to people who like your product, who are ready to value what you are selling and thus willing to pay for it when the buyer is confident he wants it. Demonstration does exactly that; it establishes the desire to acquire by creating a feeling of 'I have seen it, I want it.'

Some buyers buy without a need for a demonstration; this will primarily occur when he is already aware or have been supported to take a decision to buy what you are selling. The danger here is that he has a perception and value created by someone else and not by you, so the question you have to ask yourself is, Does he value you? He has not seen the demonstration of the product through you, so he does not value what a salesman brings into the engagement. However, if a salesman demonstrates it, it not only establishes the desire to buy but also supports the decision to buy from the salesman.

The million-dollar question is, what are one or two things you should demonstrate which will capture the attention of your buyer, the next two things you will demonstrate that will make your buyer say that 'He knows what I want', then the other two things which will make your buyer say 'This is what I want', and the last two you will demonstrate that your buyer will say 'I might want this too'? Your demonstration to the buyer should cover what he must have, what is good to have, and what is nice to have, and each time it should be complemented by *why he should buy.*

Demonstration should be engrossing; it should be like your buyer is watching a movie. Tell the story as you would want to listen to one, the one you remembered always. The product you demonstrate to your buyer has a big story in that there is a story of you, there is a story of the organization you represent, there is a story of your product, and there is a story of other buyers who bought from you—there is always a story. If you are not telling it, maybe you just do not know it. If you know, tell it enthusiastically; maybe your buyer is hearing it for the first time, but he definitely is hearing it for the first time from *you.*

While the buyer will watch the product which you are demonstrating, what he will hear is the story you tell. The combination of the story you tell and what he sees in your product is demonstration; if he finds his thrill, if he finds what he is looking for, and if he hears what he has been wanting to, he will make his decision to buy.

Know your story, practice your story, believe in your story, and say it heartily, and you will have your buyer affirming his purchase by demonstrating his acknowledgement with his body movements, showing gestures and expressions of 'I want it', which is the agreement to buy.

Demonstration should be dramatic—that is, it has to be contextual and theatrical. It should have emotions, comedy, surprises, and climax; it should be live and should feel real. Make your buyer feel your product and make him touch your product, then it should either have a happy or even sometimes a sad ending; in the end the buyer has to say, 'Wow!'

The enthusiasm while demonstrating and the theatrics while demonstrating has to be so high that your buyer at the end should give you a standing ovation or even a sign of confidence. The execution of the entire episode should give you the confidence and ability to say, 'The buyer will buy my product, or he will buy none!'

Benefits

So when we engage with our buyers, we listen for any potential for what he is or could be looking for; we demonstrate what we have to offer in context to the potential evaluated. When your buyer experiences these episodes of engagement, he is moving towards a decision to buy, but what seals the deal? What does the buyer want to hear? What does he want to match it against? What will justify his decision to buy? The answer is simple—benefits!

We need to engage with our buyers and state the benefits of the product we are selling. Everyone wants to evaluate the returns of expense, and the only way to bring arithmetic value paid for your product versus value received by the buyer is by stating benefits and the potential value of each benefit to your buyer.

What you see around you is not the statements of benefits but that the engagement has degenerated to the pitch of selling features. Feature based shopping happens when the decision to purchase is already made; in feature selling, the product is not sold but is being bought. Feature richness is exposed when your product is being bought in comparison and you mostly are competing.

The buyers do not buy features and are also unable to place arithmetical value to features; the building of features has cost you, and the buyer believes, 'Why should I pay for what you have made an expense for?' What he wants to pay for is what he needs and what will benefit him.

Convert your feature-based pitches to simple statements of benefits; the name of features should only be treated as internal code words or words which should be used as titles for making benefit statements. Let us take an example here. Let us say you are selling a shirt, blue in colour, non-iron, and in any size. I think this is an example enough, and any product can be replaced by the three characteristics of the item so it is identified with its purpose, a visible characteristic being its colour and non-iron being its feature.

Now a feature-based pitch will be (and to keep the pitch a little bland and simple): 'I have a shirt with a beautiful hue of blue and has a unique feature new in the market—it is non-iron.'

The benefit-oriented pitch will be: 'I have a lovely shirt with a beautiful hue of blue. While blue will suit you so much, what makes it unique is that you do not require to iron it. If you travel or are dressing up hurriedly every day, this is what you need, a shirt which does not require ironing at all and looks good on you too. Needless to say, the effort of ironing or the cost of ironing is saved too.'

The benefit here will be established by the buyer himself: 'It saves me effort, it saves me time, and it saves me money while it does everything else.' Every product, if you try to find out, has benefits attached; that is why it is able to compete or bring change in the buyers' usage and needs. We need to discover the benefit statement of our product or, while innovating products, clearly mark the benefit statements to pitch to our buyers, what the salesman needs to know. He needs to ask and train himself to state the benefit statement to the buyer of the product.

The benefit statement does not only establish value with your buyer; it also makes your product affordable. The buyer is able to establish its worth. With the benefits stated, the price suddenly becomes reasonable for the buyer to pay, yes, provided he can afford to pay in real terms, and now this is not a battle you can fight or convince your buyer to buy now. What you can do though is establish the desire to buy; the buyer agrees with the benefits and value and decides that he will buy when he can. The other benefit is that he might not buy now but will surely know someone who he knows can buy, and your engagement will allow him to pitch your product to this person who he knows would need such a product.

Do not sell features of your product, but make statements of benefits on every feature which your product has; the buyers will buy benefits and not the pitch of features. Features only confuse your buyers!

Negotiating

Negotiation is an attitude required in a salesman, due to which many have to abandon making sales as a career, another is striking a conversation with strangers, and the last is accepting rejection. We are right now discussing the attitude of 'asking for payment and thus preparing to negotiate'.

'If you make the payment, I can organize for delivery right away.' It is the most dreaded statement; in addition, the damn statement is designed to come after all the hard work is done and it is time for getting rewarded. This is the seal-the-deal situation; here the suspense is broken— he loves me, he loves me not; will the sale happen or not happen?

The buyer needs to pay for your product. As long as he believes he is parting with something more valuable than what he is getting in exchange, the chances of 'I do want your product' is high. I am sure after all that you have read, learnt, and practiced that the chances of rejection are bleak. If he wants it, he will buy it.

However, the last knot in the stitch is the delight of your buyer, his concern over whether he is paying the right price and whether he can get a better price, and here comes negotiation.

'What is my price? What is the discount you will offer?' is the question you fear. 'Will someone else get rewarded for your effort if he gets a better price elsewhere?' is what gives you goose bumps.

Let us understand the clean difference between asking a discount and asking for more value. *Discount* is the most common and abused word. You clearly know what you want, and thus you are now looking for the best price. However, in the case where the products are sold, it is not about the discount but the best value the buyer can get for every dollar spent. The buyer is using the word *discount* and thus bargaining; what he is actually looking for is to negotiate with you, to maximise the value of the purchase out of you. He wants clarity on whether he is missing something that he is not getting and others would have gotten. This is the conviction your buyer is looking for, and we have to be prepared to overcome it and be ready to negotiate!

Asking for a discount and giving a discount can be attributed to bargaining; it even becomes worse when you make purchases from the street. It is also known as haggling. In an environment of selling, bargaining (aka haggling) needs to be replaced with negotiation. While the buyer rightfully asks for the best price, we are required to state how we are already asking for a very low price for the product(s) worth. The discussion has to move from price to services you will ensure, the promise of after-sales service you will provide and facilitate.

The value you are required to build is that while you will not reduce the price, what after-sales service you will provide or can provide will make it worth the buyer's while to buy; the value should delight your buyer and should ensure that he is also like any other buyer of yours, who will get the best value for every dollar paid to you.

Bargaining and discounting should be discouraged, but relationship and negotiation should be encouraged.

Offer a giveaway, which makes the offer compelling for the buyer to buy, and hold it close to your chest till the discussion comes to the paying for the product you are selling. Sometimes you give it away because 'I want more' was asked, and sometimes you will give it away not because it was asked but because you value such relationships with buyers who trust you for the value you ask for and deliver.

After the giveaway, the final element has to be a trade-off. If your buyer wants even more, he becomes stubborn and insists, then you should be willing to give more, but by taking away from him, it is commonly known in the world of business as a trade-off.

A trade-off is something that you are willing to part with for something in return. You should have this too closely held to your chest. By trade-off, you will send a clear message that now you are going to take away things from your product to meet the insistence of your buyer.

If trade-off is invoked by you and offered to the buyer and if your buyer finds worth, he will take your offer; if yes, or even if no, the chances are that the deal will be sealed and product sold.

If not, there is always someone else, some other time, someplace else. The ocean is full of potential, if you are a salesman!

If you apply, practice, and overcome the ten barriers, you will be the *salesman*!

Index

About the Author

He has twenty-one and more years of sales experience in SMEs in India and the Middle East.

His knowledge & experience comes from working with a technology company pioneering in productized solutions for businesses, with possibly the largest network of sales across India.

Deepak is happily married to Nandita for the past sixteen years, has a caring son, Dhairya, and a pretty daughter, Laavanya, and they reside with his mother, Suman, at Bangalore.

About
Break the Barriers of Selling

This series of self-help articles is based on experiences of the author; it exposes the differences between a customer when he buys and when the customer is sold to.

These articles are written so as to prepare the salesman who engages to sell in reaching out to his prospective customer and establish the beginning of a relationship between the salesman and the buyer, taking pride in who he sells to and the repute of what he sells—all in all, a hero of everyone.

Any salesperson engaged in selling products and services which require needs to be established, selling new products which require the prospects to be found, the products to be demonstrated to sell will identify with the articles and can make the best out of it to learn or to refresh themselves.

This compilation also guides the salesperson to develop himself in selling.